CLASSICAL THEMES FOR TWO

Arrangements by Peter Deneff

ISBN 978-1-5400-1415-3

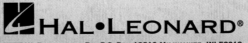

7777 W. BLUEMOUND RD. P.O. BOX 13819 MILWAUKEE, WI 53213

In Australia Contact:
Hal Leonard Australia Pty. Ltd.
4 Lentara Court
Cheltenham, Victoria, 3192 Australia
Email: ausadmin@halleonard.com.au

Copyright © 2017 by HAL LEONARD LLC
International Copyright Secured   All Rights Reserved

For all works contained herein:
Unauthorized copying, arranging, adapting, recording, Internet posting, public performance,
or other distribution of the printed music in this publication is an infringement of copyright.
Infringers are liable under the law.

Visit Hal Leonard Online at
www.halleonard.com

ACADEMIC FESTIVAL OVERTURE

TROMBONES

By JOHANNES BRAHMS

Allegro

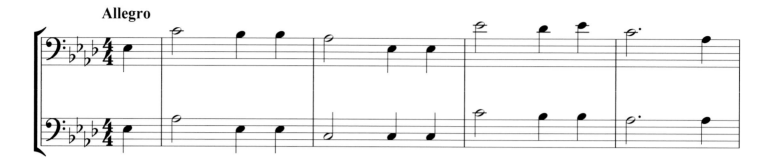

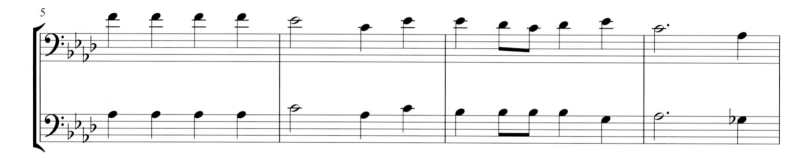

Copyright © 2017 by HAL LEONARD LLC
International Copyright Secured   All Rights Reserved

AIR
from WATER MUSIC

TROMBONES

By GEORGE FRIDERIC HANDEL

Andante con moto

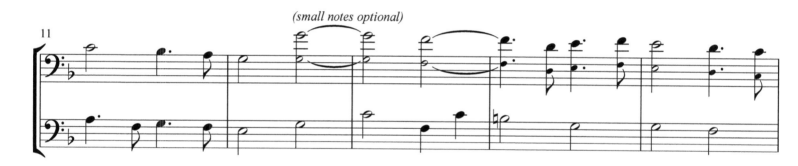

(small notes optional)

Copyright © 2017 by HAL LEONARD LLC
International Copyright Secured   All Rights Reserved

AIR ON THE G STRING
from ORCHESTRAL SUITE NO. 3 IN D MAJOR, BWV 1068

TROMBONES

By JOHANN SEBASTIAN BACH

Adagio

Copyright © 2017 by HAL LEONARD LLC
International Copyright Secured   All Rights Reserved

BLUE DANUBE WALTZ

TROMBONES

By JOHANN STRAUSS, JR.

Copyright © 2017 by HAL LEONARD LLC
International Copyright Secured   All Rights Reserved

CANON IN D

TROMBONES

By JOHANN PACHELBEL

Moderately

Copyright © 2017 by HAL LEONARD LLC
International Copyright Secured   All Rights Reserved

CLAIR DE LUNE
from SUITE BERGAMASQUE

TROMBONES

By CLAUDE DEBUSSY

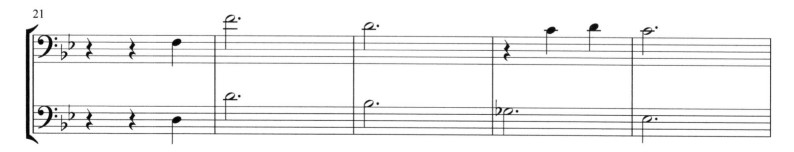

Copyright © 2017 by HAL LEONARD LLC
International Copyright Secured   All Rights Reserved

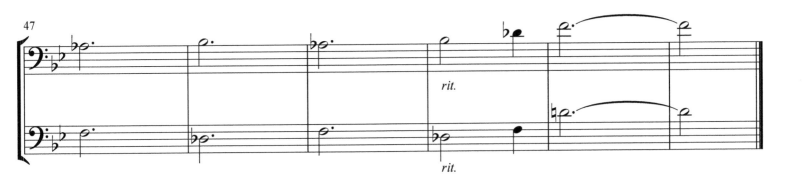

EINE KLEINE NACHTMUSIK
(Second Movement Theme: "Romance")

TROMBONES

By WOLFGANG AMADEUS MOZART

Andante

Copyright © 2017 by HAL LEONARD LLC
International Copyright Secured   All Rights Reserved

FLOWER DUET
from LAKMÉ

TROMBONES

By LÉO DELIBES

Andante con moto

Copyright © 2017 by HAL LEONARD LLC
International Copyright Secured   All Rights Reserved

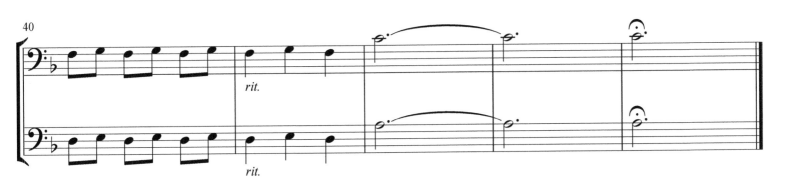

HALLELUJAH CHORUS
from MESSIAH

TROMBONES

By GEORGE FRIDERIC HANDEL

Allegro

Copyright © 2017 by HAL LEONARD LLC
International Copyright Secured   All Rights Reserved

(small note optional)

HORNPIPE
from WATER MUSIC

TROMBONES

By GEORGE FRIDERIC HANDEL

Allegro maestoso

Copyright © 2017 by HAL LEONARD LLC
International Copyright Secured   All Rights Reserved

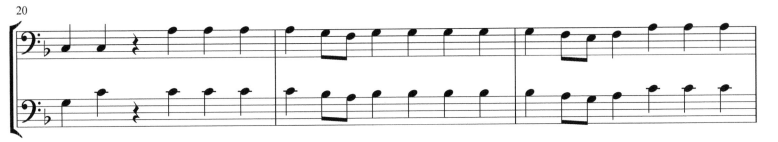

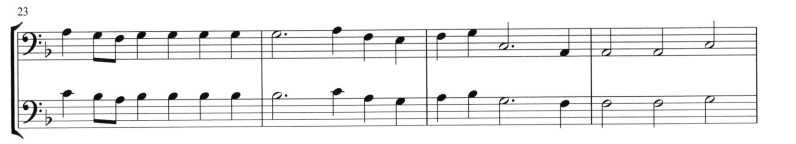

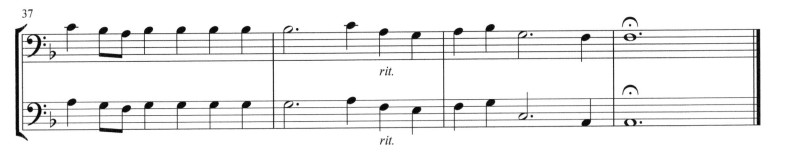

HUNGARIAN DANCE NO. 5

TROMBONES

By JOHANNES BRAHMS

Allegro

Copyright © 2017 by HAL LEONARD LLC
International Copyright Secured   All Rights Reserved

25

To Coda ⊕

29

34

39

44

1.

2.

D.C. al Coda

CODA
⊕

49
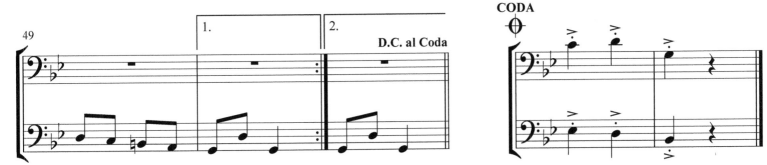

JESU, JOY OF MAN'S DESIRING

from CANTATA 147

TROMBONES

By JOHANN SEBASTIAN BACH

Moderately

Copyright © 2017 by HAL LEONARD LLC
International Copyright Secured   All Rights Reserved

D.C. al Coda

CODA

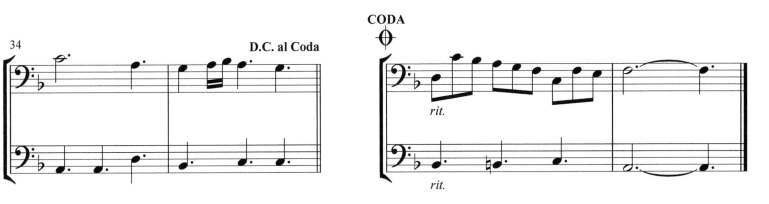

rit.

MARCH
from THE NUTCRACKER

TROMBONES

By PYOTR IL'YICH TCHAIKOVSKY

March tempo

Copyright © 2017 by HAL LEONARD LLC
International Copyright Secured   All Rights Reserved

MINUET IN G
from ANNA MAGDALENA NOTEBOOK

TROMBONES

By CHRISTIAN PETZOLD
formerly attributed to J.S. Bach

Copyright © 2017 by HAL LEONARD LLC
International Copyright Secured   All Rights Reserved

ODE TO JOY

from SYMPHONY NO. 9 IN D MINOR

TROMBONES

By LUDWIG VAN BEETHOVEN

Allegro

rit.

rit.

Copyright © 2017 by HAL LEONARD LLC
International Copyright Secured   All Rights Reserved

MORNING
from PEER GYNT

By EDVARD GRIEG

TROMBONES

Allegretto pastorale

Copyright © 2017 by HAL LEONARD LLC
International Copyright Secured   All Rights Reserved

PICTURES AT AN EXHIBITION
(Promenade)

TROMBONES

By MODEST MUSSORGSKY

Copyright © 2017 by HAL LEONARD LLC
International Copyright Secured   All Rights Reserved

POMP AND CIRCUMSTANCE
March No. 1

TROMBONES

By EDWARD ELGAR

Allegro

Copyright © 2017 by HAL LEONARD LLC
International Copyright Secured   All Rights Reserved

RONDEAU
from SUITE DE SYMPHONIE

TROMBONES

By JEAN-JOSEPH MOURET

Moderately

Copyright © 2017 by HAL LEONARD LLC
International Copyright Secured   All Rights Reserved

SHEEP MAY SAFELY GRAZE

from CANTATA 208

TROMBONES

By JOHANN SEBASTIAN BACH

Andante

5

9

13

18

Copyright © 2017 by HAL LEONARD LLC
International Copyright Secured   All Rights Reserved

THE SURPRISE SYMPHONY
(Symphony No. 94, Second Movement Theme)

TROMBONES

By FRANZ JOSEPH HAYDN

Andante

Copyright © 2017 by HAL LEONARD LLC
International Copyright Secured   All Rights Reserved

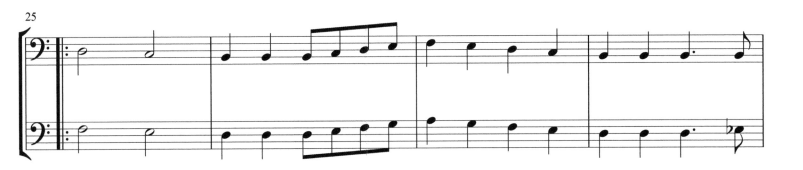

SYMPHONY NO. 7
(Second Movement Theme)

TROMBONES

By LUDWIG VAN BEETHOVEN

Allegretto

Copyright © 2017 by HAL LEONARD LLC
International Copyright Secured   All Rights Reserved

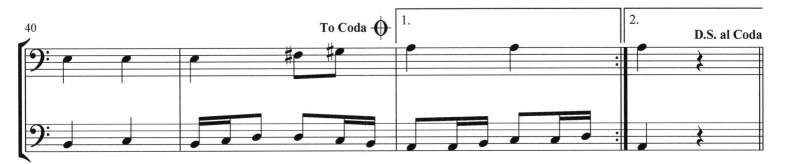

TRUMPET VOLUNTARY
(Prince of Denmark's March)

TROMBONES

By JEREMIAH CLARKE

Moderately

Copyright © 2017 by HAL LEONARD LLC
International Copyright Secured   All Rights Reserved

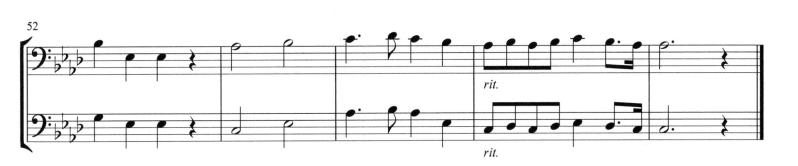

WILLIAM TELL OVERTURE
(Theme)

TROMBONES

By GIOACHINO ROSSINI

Copyright © 2017 by HAL LEONARD LLC
International Copyright Secured   All Rights Reserved

HAL LEONARD PRESENTS

EASY INSTRUMENTAL DUETS

Start your duet playing experience with these fun songbooks! Over 20 easy duet arrangements for two instrumentalists are featured in each of these collections. Woodwind and brass editions can be played together as can the string editions.

THE BEATLES FOR TWO

23 favorites from the Fab Four in easy duet arrangements for two instrumentalists are featured in this collection: All You Need Is Love • Eleanor Rigby • Here Comes the Sun • Hey Jude • I Want to Hold Your Hand • Penny Lane • Something • Yellow Submarine • Yesterday • and more.

00291024	FLUTE	00291028	TROMBONE
00291025	CLARINET	00291029	VIOLIN
00291026	ALTO SAX	00291030	CELLO
00291027	TRUMPET		

BROADWAY SONGS FOR TWO

22 showstoppers: Any Dream Will Do • Bring Him Home • Cabaret • Edelweiss • For Forever • Hello, Dolly! • I Believe • Memory • One • Popular • Seasons of Love • Seventy Six Trombones • Tomorrow • Where Is Love? • You've Got a Friend • and more.

00252493	FLUTE	00252497	TROMBONE
00252494	CLARINET	00252500	VIOLIN
00252495	ALTO SAX	00252501	CELLO
00252496	TRUMPET		

CHRISTMAS CAROLS FOR TWO

Songs include: Angels We Have Heard on High • Away in a Manger • Deck the Hall • Jingle Bells • Joy to the World • O Holy Night • Silent Night • We Wish You a Merry Christmas • and more.

00277964	FLUTE	00277968	TROMBONE
00277965	CLARINET	00277969	VIOLIN
00277966	ALTO SAX	00277970	CELLO
00277967	TRUMPET		

HAL•LEONARD®

CHRISTMAS HITS FOR TWO

22 terrific holiday duets: All I Want for Christmas Is You • Baby, It's Cold Outside • The Christmas Song (Chestnuts Roasting on an Open Fire) • Do You Want to Build a Snowman? • Feliz Navidad • Have Yourself a Merry Little Christmas • It's Beginning to Look like Christmas • Let It Snow! Let It Snow! Let It Snow! • Mary, Did You Know? • Rockin' Around the Christmas Tree • Silver Bells • White Christmas • and more.

00172461	FLUTE	00172465	TROMBONE
00172462	CLARINET	00172466	VIOLIN
00172463	ALTO SAX	00172467	CELLO
00172464	TRUMPET		

CLASSIC ROCK FOR TWO

23 classic rock songs: Bang a Gong (Get It On) • Can't Fight This Feeling • Carry on Wayward Son • Cold As Ice • Come on Eileen • Come Together • Crocodile Rock • Down on the Corner • Every Little Thing She Does Is Magic • Free Fallin' • Hurts So Good • The Joker • Livin' on a Prayer • and more.

00303026	FLUTE	00303030	TROMBONE
00303027	CLARINET	00303031	VIOLIN
00303028	ALTO SAX	00303032	CELLO
00303029	TRUMPET		

CLASSICAL THEMES FOR TWO

24 favorite melodies from top classical composers: Air on the G String • Blue Danube Waltz • Canon in D • Eine Kleine Nachtmusik • Hallelujah Chorus • Jesu, Joy of Man's Desiring • Minuet in G Major • Ode to Joy • Pictures at an Exhibition • Sheep May Safely Graze • Trumpet Voluntary • William Tell Overture • and more.

00254439	FLUTE	00254443	TROMBONE
00254440	CLARINET	00254444	VIOLIN
00254441	ALTO SAX	00254445	CELLO
00254442	TRUMPET		

Prices, contents and availability subject to change without notice. Sales restrictions to some countries apply. All prices listed in U.S. funds.

DISNEY SONGS FOR TWO

23 Disney favorites: Beauty and the Beast • Circle of Life • Evermore • Friend Like Me • How Far I'll Go • Let It Go • Mickey Mouse March • Supercalifragilisticexpialidocious • When You Wish upon a Star • A Whole New World • Zip-A-Dee-Doo-Dah • and more.

00284643	FLUTE	00284647	TROMBONE
00284644	CLARINET	00284648	VIOLIN
00284645	ALTO SAX	00284649	CELLO
00284646	TRUMPET		

HIT SONGS FOR TWO

22 mega hits: All About That Bass • All of Me • Brave • Can't Stop the Feeling • Grenade • Hey, Soul Sister • I Will Wait • Let Her Go • 100 Years • Royals • Shake It Off • Shape of You • Stay with Me • Viva La Vida • and more.

00252482	FLUTE	00252486	TROMBONE
00252483	CLARINET	00252487	VIOLIN
00252484	ALTO SAX	00252488	CELLO
00252485	TRUMPET		

MOVIE SONGS FOR TWO

23 blockbuster hits are featured in this collection: City of Stars • Footloose • Hallelujah • Moon River • The Pink Panther • Puttin' on the Ritz • Skyfall • That's Amore • and more.

00284651	FLUTE	00284655	TROMBONE
00284652	CLARINET	00284656	VIOLIN
00284653	ALTO SAX	00284657	CELLO
00284654	TRUMPET		

POP CLASSICS FOR TWO

23 classic pop hits: Africa • Alone • Can't Smile Without You • Centerfold • Dancing Queen • Dust in the Wind • Every Breath You Take • Eye of the Tiger • I Melt with You • I Still Haven't Found What I'm Looking For • Imagine • Jessie's Girl • and more.

00303019	FLUTE	00303023	TROMBONE
00303020	CLARINET	00303024	VIOLIN
00303021	ALTO SAX	00303025	CELLO
00303022	TRUMPET		

ORDER TODAY AT HALLEONARD.COM

0722
508